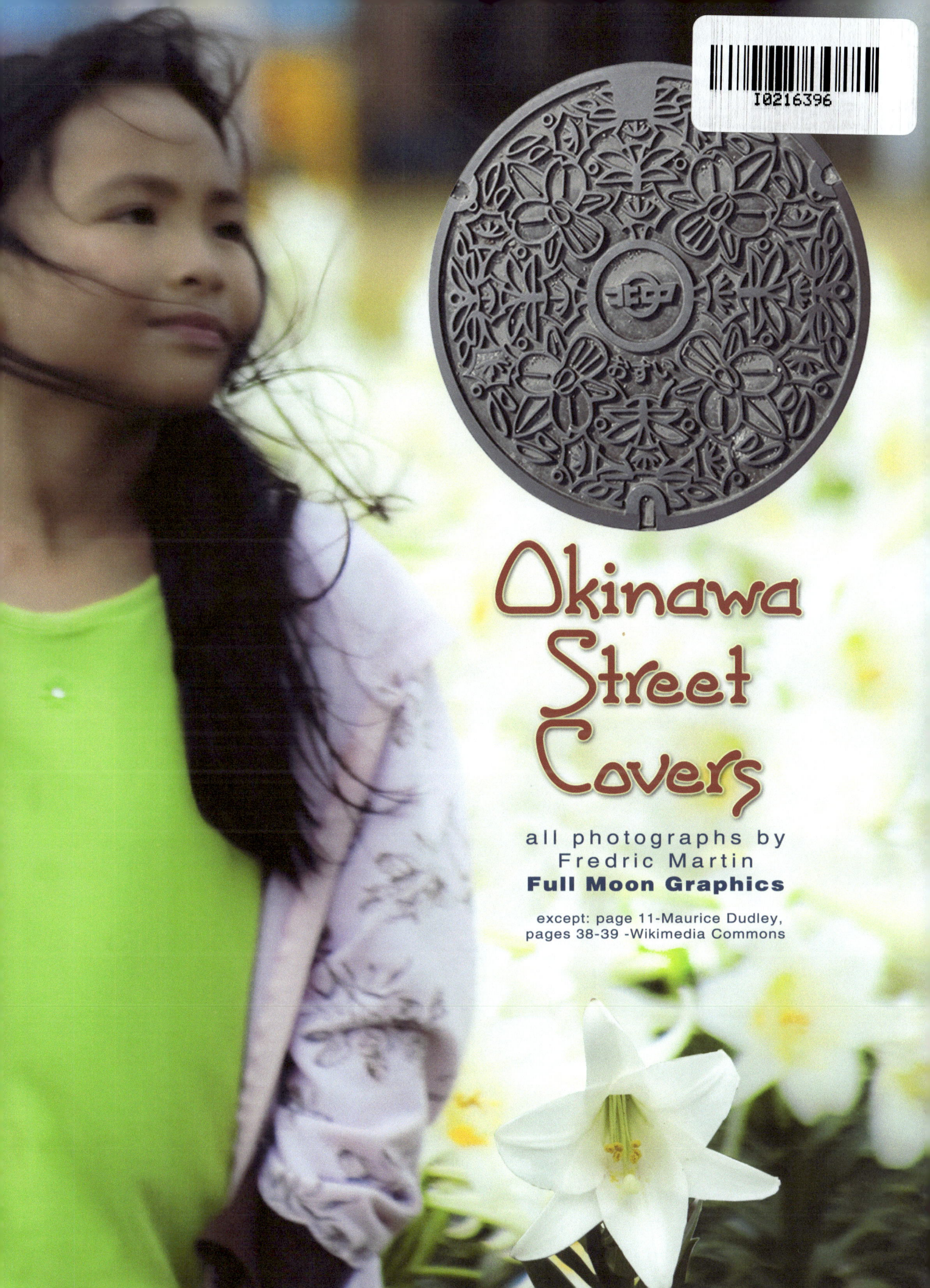

Okinawa Street Covers

all photographs by
Fredric Martin
Full Moon Graphics

except: page 11-Maurice Dudley,
pages 38-39 -Wikimedia Commons

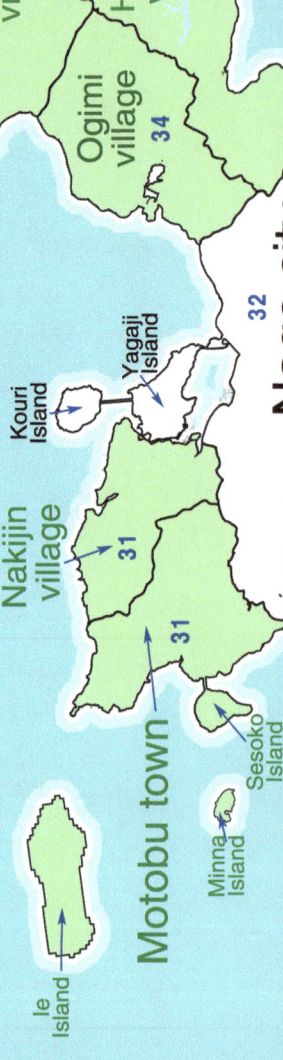

I have been fascinated by the beautiful, imaginative, and proud works of art found at my feet in Japan. I was thrilled to find these street covers (I prefer this term instead of manhole covers) in Okinawa Prefecture as well. The Prefecture of Okinawa is divided into municipalities designated as cities, towns, and villages based on population. Each town, city, and village proudly display who they are and what is significant about their community in the utilitarian, functional street covers. In recent years, when that population decreases several communities merge to form new cities. I have captured the street covers for as many of the original entities as well as covers for the new combined cities. You may see an ornately designed cover next to a seemingly identical street cover, with the only difference being that the community's symbol has changed. It has become a very exciting challenge to find each town, village, and city's homage to the things that are important to the people of that community.

Fredric Martin

Nanjo city

Miyako-jima

Ginoza village

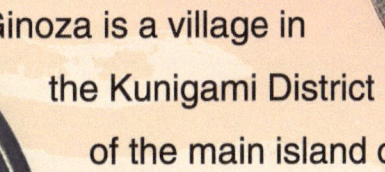

Ginoza is a village in the Kunigami District of the main island of Okinawa and is on the Pacific coast. There are many activities that occur in this village in August. There are harvest festivals and religious celebrations scheduled by the lunar calendar.

The street covers show the August Ashibi play which includes karate, comedians, and drum corps with dancers. The play began in 1896 and keeps alive their ancient Ryukyu traditions and heritage. The Japan Cultural Council has selected Ginoza's August play as one of Japan's Cultural Assets. You can see the traditional dancing lion-dog called a shishimai.

Kin town

Kin town's street cover celebrates the uniquely Okinawa three-stringed instrument called the sanshin. Sanshins are usually made out of oak or blackwood, and most are covered with python skins to amplify the sound of the strings. The three strings were traditionally made out of natural fibers such as horse hair or silk, but today they are made of synthetic fibers. That strange character to the right playing the sanshin is called a shisa. The lion-dog shisa have been around for centuries, guarding homes and keeping evil spirits away.

- 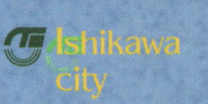 Ishikawa city
- 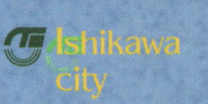 Gushikawa city
- 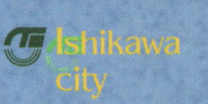 Yonashiro town
- 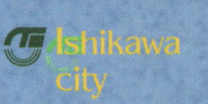 Katsuren town

Ishikawa city

 Uruma city

On April 1, 2005, the cities of Gushikawa and Ishikawa and the towns of Katsuren and Yonashiro incorporated to become Uruma city. Uruma city also includes eight Yokatsu Islands. This area is famous for the unique style of bullfights. They are not like bullfights in Spain with matadors. In Uruma, the bulls square off against each other, somewhat like sumo wrestlers. The winning bull becomes the yokozuna, the grand champion. The name "*Uruma*" comes from an archaic name in the Ryukyu language for coral (*uru*) and island (*ma*).

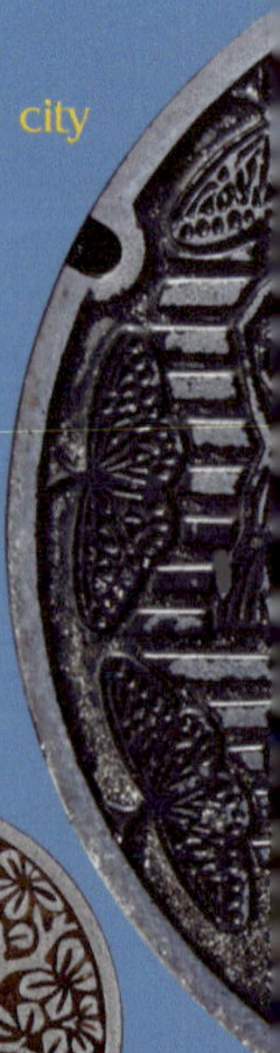

Uruma city

Katsuren

Ishikawa city

Gushikawa city

Gushikawa city

Yonashiro

Okinawa City

Okinawa City is the second largest city in Okinawa Prefecture. It is located in the center of the main island of Okinawa. With a population of over 128,000, Okinawa City has a density of 2620 persons per square kilometer.

In 1956, the village of Goeku changed its name to Koza. On July 1 of that year it became a city. On April 1, 1974, Okinawa City was founded by the merger of Koza and Misato.

The street cover of Okinawa City shows the beautiful hibiscus flowers which can be seen everywhere in the city, and the Chinese fan palm or fountain palm (scientific name **Livistona chinensis**), which is called **birou** in Japanese.

Kitanakagusuku

Kitanakagusuku is a World Heritage site of one of the Ryukyu Kingdom castle ruins dating back to the 15th century. "*Gusuku*" were Ryukyu Kingdom castles built as early as the fourteenth century with long winding walls. "*Kita*" means north and "*Naka*" means central. Orchids are the official flowers of the village of Kitanakagusuku.

Nakagusuku village

The street covers of this mid-island village show the ancient walls of the Nakagusuku castle, whose ruins lie on the border with the neighboring village of Kitanakagusuku. These hard, strong walls are in direct contrast to the delicate beauty around them, represented by the hibiscus blossoms.

The town of Nishihara is called "Education Town" because the University of the Ryukyus and the Okinawa Christian Junior College are located in Nishihara, and the Okinawa International University is located nearby. The street covers show the flowering tree the Japanese call *sagarabana* (which means "dangling flower"). In English, the common name is the powderpuff tree (*Barringtonia racemosa*).

Nishihara town

🌷 Haebaru town

The town of Haebaru celebrates the fine art of weaving in their street covers. Okinawa has always been known for the beautiful and creative woven fabrics such as **bashofu**, resist dye art called **bingata**, fabric dyes called **kasuri**, and garments made from banana fibers called **Shuri** weave. Shuri weave is named for the capital of the Ryukyu Kingdom which is now part of Haebaru town and Naha, the current capital. It is easy to see why these gorgeous textile products have become so popular. There is a Prefecture School for the Blind in Haebaru, and it is suggested that the person at the loom is blind. Haebaru town is the only municipality on the Island of Okinawa that does not have any coastline.

Yonabaru

The people in the town of Yonabaru have their own version of the tug-of-war game called **Yonabaru Tsunahiki**. In Yonabaru the fishermen on one side and the farmers on the other participate in this gigantic version of the tug-of-war contest to see who will win and secure good luck for their harvest. It is amazing to watch and even more amazing to participate in pulling the 90 meter, five-ton rope. *Tsunahiki* has been a traditional part of their lives for over 400 years.

photo by Maurice Dudley

Nanjo city

Golf is very popular in Okinawa. There are a great many driving ranges and courses throughout the islands. This is the famous Ryukyu Golf Club which has three 27-hole courses.

Tamagusuku village

On January 1, 2006, the town of Sashiki and the villages of Tamagusuku, Chinen, and Ozato merged to form the new city of Nanjo. Nanjo is on the Pacific side of Okinawa island on the southern end.

Ozato village

Nanjo city

The villages of Ozato, Chinen, and Tamagusuku, and the town of Sashiki merged on January 1, 2006, to form Nanjo city. The tree on the Ozato street cover (above) and now on the Nanjo city cover (right) may be a stylized tree from a sacred grove where only royalty were allowed to go, or it may be an ebony tree, the symbolic tree of Nanjo. The flowers (same as the Haebaru design) may be hibiscus, the official flowers of Nanjo. The tree is the same design as the one on the Ishikawa (Uruma) cover (see page 4). The lady in the photo is a street vendor selling bento lunch boxes.

Chinen village

Chinen (pronounced *shi-nen*) village, which is now part of Nanjo city, is a glorious place on the southeast Pacific coast of Okinawa. The street covers found there depict the blue sky and green waters that Okinawa is famous for. They also show the lilies and shining beaches found everywhere in Okinawa. Chinen village's logo represents the Sêfa-utaki, a most unusual natural site that was once a sacred altar, where entry was limited to the royal government of the Ryukyu Kingdom. Today everyone may visit this beautiful spot that is listed as a UNESCO World Cultural and National Heritage site.

O Island

O Island, off the Pacific coast of Okinawa Island, is a tiny village that was a part of Tamagusuku and is now a part of Nanjo City.

Sashiki village

Sashiki village is another village that is now a section of Nanjo city. These creatures are mudskippers, amphibious fish that use their pectoral fins to walk on land. They look similar to the shisa good-luck creatures with one fish's mouth open and the other's mouth closed.

Kochinda town

Kochinda was a town located in Shimajiri District (southern Okinawa Island). It merged with Gushikami in 2006 to become Yaese town.

Agriculture is a major livelihood in Yaese. Much of the southern area of Okinawa island is farm land. It is amazing how a drink or cigarette vending machine can always be found in the middle of the sugarcane fields.

Yaese town

🌀 Gushikami village

Gushikami was a village in the Shimajiri District of Okinawa. On January 1, 2006, Gushikami merged with the town of Kochinda to form the new town of Yaese. The flower of Gusgikami village was the lily. Fishing was the main industry of Gushikami, and still is in Yaese. One important food crop is a species of flying fish which has become the symbol of the village.

A traditional dance called **Shi-ya-ma** was performed by Shinjo village girls for the Ryukyu king at Shuri Castle in 1839. The king, Shoiku, was so impressed that he gave his stables and farm to the villagers. In 1994, the dance was designated as an important cultural asset, and the memorial was erected to commemorate the event. The street cover shows a Shi-ya-ma dancer and the farm animals given to the villagers.

Itoman city

Itoman city, the southern-most area of the main island of Okinawa, hosts an annual tug-of-war and parade, called **Tsunahiki**. Thousands participate each year to wish for a good harvest and prosperous fishing. Many towns have similar events.

Tomigusuku city

The best word to describe Tomigusuku is diversity, as represented by the photo of the stone sculptures below. Tomigusuku is a populated city adjacent to the capital of Naha to its north and open farmland to the south. The visitor will be surprised to see a modern monorail transit system and very chic fashion outlets in Tomigusuku. But the visitor will also find a wetland wildlife preserve and beautiful beaches facing the East China Sea. One can see ancient religious ceremonies and current rock concerts. Events on the city calendar include Haarii Yurai Matsuri (Dragon Boat Origin Festival), The 15th Ujizome Matsuri (Sugar cane Dyeing Festival), Oyaji Love Rock Festival, and the Castle Utaki Tomigusuku Festival.

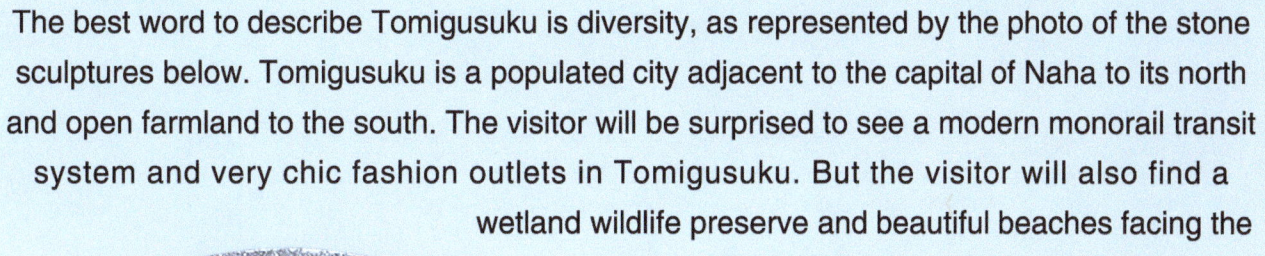

Naha city

The capital of Okinawa Prefecture, Naha is a modern port city with a population of 317,906 (December 31, 2009 census). **Naha-te** or **Nawate**, a martial art developed in Naha together with martial arts styles developed in Tomari and Shuri, formed the basis for **Okinawa-te**, which in turn is the origin of today's karate. Naha is the location of Shuri Castle, a restored Ryukyu Kingdom site that was destroyed during World War II and has been completely rebuilt. During the Naha Festival in the Fall, the world's largest tug-of-war, documented in the *"Guinness World Records,"* is held here.

Urasoe city

This city has a proud history and was the capital of the Ryukyu Kingdom from 1187 to 1405. The name **Urasoe** derived from "**ura osou**" which means "to dominate" and has remained unchanged since Okinawa's earliest time. Urasoe is called "**Tedako no Mach**i" which means "the city of the sun child." Urasoe, designated city-status on July 1,1970, holds an annual Tedako Matsuri festival in July.

Ginowan city

Ginowan was completely destroyed during the Battle of Okinawa (WWII) with some of the heaviest fighting occurring here. But the city has made steady recovery and prospered due to agriculture, small businesses and industry. U. S. Marine Corps Air Station Futenma is in Ginowan, though some residents would appreciate it if they moved on. The Okinawa Convention Center is in Ginowan.

Chatan town

Chatan is a town on the West coast of Okinawa Island, the East China Sea. It is a narrow community along Highway 58 which runs north and south parallel to the man-made coastline. The initials "CCZ" stand for Coastal Community Zone.

The street covers show the surf and beaches that make Chatan a popular place. Three of the six districts attract a lot of businesses and coastal recreation: Kitamae, Mihama, and Sunabe. The other three districts, Kamiseido, Ihei, and Kuwae, are mostly residential.

Beniimo (purple sweet potato) is a popular flavor of ice cream and other sweets. Sweet potatoes are best served hot on the street

Kadena town

Noguni Soukan, who worked as a manager of trade for the Ryukyu government, brought some sweet potato plants from China in 1605. He grew them in the Noguni district of Kadena town. He taught Gima Shinjo, who lived in Kaki-no-hana village (Futenma now) to grow sweet potatoes and they were cultivated all over the Ryukyu Islands. Noguni Soukan is called "*Umu-Ufushu*" (Sir Sweet Potato). Today Okinawa is well-known for its purple sweet potato, which originated in the Americas. Purple ***beniimo*** sweet potatoes are a large part of the Okinawan diet. They even have beniimo-flavored ice cream and cookies. In cooler months, you can find vendors selling hot sweet potatoes in small trucks. They play musical bells , similar to the ice cream trucks in the United States. Kadena town has a popular sweet potato festival every year.

It is logical to expect a large number of Okinawa municipalities and islands to show ocean and nautical scenes in their street cover art.

Yomitan has a long naval history because of its central location on the East China Sea. Yomitan's coast has many popular diving locations.

Onna is a resort village and artists' community.

Motobu is a fishing port town in the north of Okinawa island and the location of Churaumi Aquarium (the third largest in the world) at Ocean Expo Park.

Nakijin is the site of one of the gusuku castle ruins.

Zamami Island (part of the Kerama Islands) is a popular location to see humpback whales.

My apologies to Master Katsushika Hokusai-san for the blatant commercial misuse of his artwork

 Yomitan village

 Onna village

Motobu town Nakijin village Zamami Island

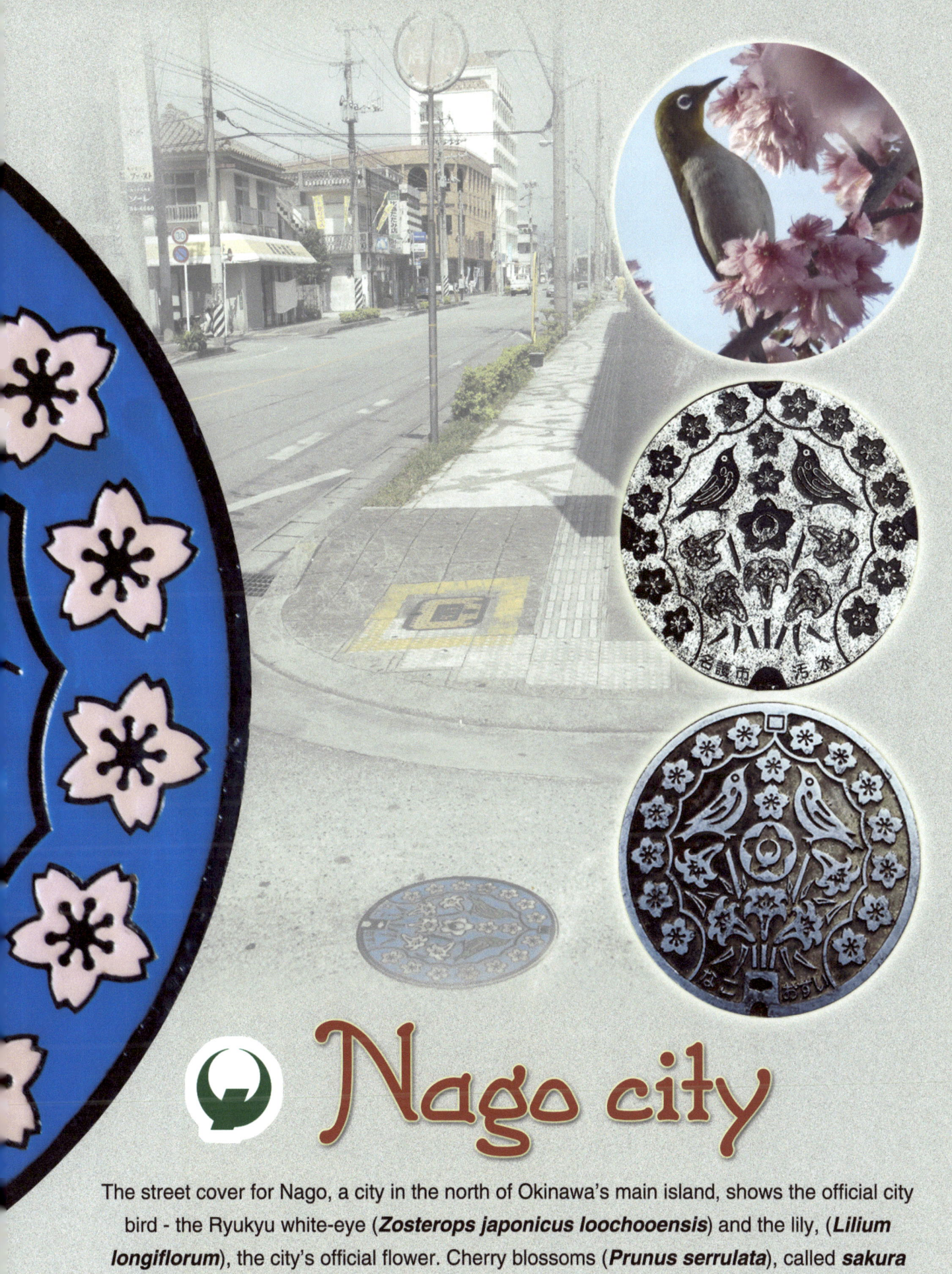

Nago city

The street cover for Nago, a city in the north of Okinawa's main island, shows the official city bird - the Ryukyu white-eye (*Zosterops japonicus loochooensis*) and the lily, (*Lilium longiflorum*), the city's official flower. Cherry blossoms (*Prunus serrulata*), called **sakura** are shown around the outer rim. Nago hosts a popular cherry blossom festival in February.

Ogimi village

Ogimi village is on the East China Sea (west) coast of Okinawa Island. Hiking to Hiji Falls is a popular recreation, along with the many water sports.

☀ Higashi village

Kayaking on the Gesashi River in the mangrove forest is only one of many recreational activities possible in the northern area of Higashi village. Okinawa has protected a large part of its natural resources while allowing people to enter and experience these beautiful sites.

◄ Kunigami village

Hedo Point offers breathtaking scenes in this nature-protected area at the northern tip of Okinawa Island.

Gusukube town

Miyako Island

Hirara City

Shimoji town

The city of Hirara and the towns of Gusukube and Shimoji merged with the village of Ueno to form the new city of Miyakojima in 2005.
The Hirara cover depicts the Strong Man athletic competition held on Miyako Island annually.
The cover found in Shimoji shows the rare breed of ponies that originated on Miyako Island.
The street cover at left shows the lighthouse at Cape Higashi-hennazaki and the wild lilies that bloom each year at this nationally-designated "Place of Scenic Beauty."

Miyakojima

Hateruma Island

Hateruma is an island in the Yaeyama District of Okinawa Prefecture, Japan, and is part of the town of Taketomi. Hateruma is 12.7 square kilometers, composed of coral, and has approximate 600 inhabitants. It is the southern-most inhabited island in Japan at 24°2'25" north latitude, 123°47'16" east longitude. Its southern location makes it one of the few places in Japan where the Southern Cross can be observed.

Iheya village

Iheya village is on small sliver of an island north of the main island of Okinawa. One of the most famous residents of this island is a very old Ryukyu umbrella pine tree shown on their street covers (below).

Aguni village

Aguni village is west of Okinawa island. Aguni is a lush semi-tropical island with beautiful plants, such as the cycad sago palm (*Cycas revoluta*).

Ishigaki city

Ishigaki was founded in 1908 as Yaeyama village when the original village of Ishigaki, and the villages of Ohama, and Miyara merged. It grew to be called Ishigaki village in 1914; and became a town in 1926. And then on July 10, 1947 it became a city. The street covers of Ishigaki show the city's official flower, Sakishima tsutsuji (*Rhododendron amanoi Ohwi*).

www.ingramcontent.com/pod-product-compliance
Lightning Source LLC
Chambersburg PA
CBHW041225040426

42444CB00002B/43